Anatomy of Letters Unsent

OrangeBooks Publication

1st Floor, Rajhans Arcade, Mall Road, Kohka, Bhilai, Chhattisgarh 490020
Website: **www.orangebooks.in**

© Copyright, 2024, Author

All rights reserved. No part of this book may be reproduced, stored in a retrieval system, or transmitted, in any form by any means, electronic, mechanical, magnetic, optical, chemical, manual, photocopying, recording or otherwise, without the prior written consent of its writer.

First Edition, 2024

ISBN: 978-93-6554-891-4

THE
anatomy
OF LETTERS UNSENT

ANVITA BHOGADI

OrangeBooks Publication
www.orangebooks.in

Author's Note

when i flipped through countless poetry collections, i noticed the pattern of themes going from hurting, heartbreak and loss to polar opposites of self-care, happiness and miracles. but is that actually how life works? aren't the ups and downs a vicious cycle that keep repeating one after the other? i've never been one to be satisfied with the ordinance and that is what led me to make this book work differently. life's a learning process and a million quotes in, you'll find that it doesn't always stay constant. i wanted the thematics to match the route of life, and as corny as it sounded, i wanted to stick by it.

tween angst, covid, board year anxiety, heart pitfalling into my stomach and a whole set of mundane issues — here's a little (huge) part of my life; moments where i smiled, cried, lay exhausted, cried again and laughed my heart out.

this is a compilation of my works from twelve, thirteen, fourteen and a little part of fifteen. as i move forward with experimenting new themes and styles, it's only right to put forth all i've written to reach where i am now. this one's for the little girl in me. the one who dreamed enough and trusted the future to make it happen

to ammamma and tatagaru; mom and dad
  — the first loves of my life

Introduction

disclaimer: i've never really been in love, not seriously.

but every action of mine is driven by love – majorly platonic you can't not love warmth

surrounded by the people who i never thought would show up; as i write this book, i'm slowly being loved back the way i love through art, film, poetry and email

but that's a story for another collection

contents

1	**tuesday tests and class of '23 core**		**1**
	i.	introduction	**2**
		a. *my favourite mode of transport is memories*	*3*
		b. *mid examination epiphanies*	*4*
		c. *class of '23*	*5*
		d. *midsummer march*	*6*
		e. *shakespearean vows*	*7*
		f. *to live is to leave*	*9*
2	**death by a thousand cuts**		**11**
	ii.	introduction	**12**
		a. *flashbacks from my future waking me up*	*12*
		b. *untitled.mp4 (2022)*	*14*
		c. *adulting fantasies*	*15*
		d. *call me by my name*	*16*
		e. *you're an equation i can never derive*	*17*
		f. *tales from my worn out honda city*	*18*

- g. grad 19
- h. old friends after summer died blue 20
- i. to may, we were bestfriends 21
- j. i don't like eternal spring 22
- k. letting go but staying true 23
- l. slipping away 24
- m. scream queens 26
- n. rational (until proven irrational) fears ... 27

3 midnight swim 28
iii. introduction 29

- a. therapy from a swim session 29
- b. ancestral visions 30
- c. two lilacs in the corner slowly growing apart 31
- d. two lilacs 31
- e. hey, remember our concrete jungle filled with dreams? 32
- f. vatican night 33
- g. she taught me women can be cruel too 34
- h. tumblr girls (2021) // art museum thoughts 35
- i. my entire personality is just longing for old friends and forgive but not forget 36

- j. sides 37
- k. one evening with the waves 38
- l. once upon a midnight spark 39
- m. secrets of the moon 40
- n. garden of time 41
- o. the night sky didn't help me write (writer's block in a midnight age) 43
- p. my sleep cycle's as messed as you 44

4   5:43pm 45
iv.   introduction 46
- a. sunsets in a modern age 46
- b. lavender blossoms 47
- c. my subconscious lingers for way too long 48
- d. falling out of love 50
- e. i still love you 51
- f. home away from home? 54
- g. august slipped away 55
- h. september tears and april fears 56
- i. looped 57
- j. only in october 58
- k. it doesn't matter anymore but back then it really did 59

	l.	*circle moment* 60
	m.	*grieving friendships* 61
	n.	*grieving friendships pt. 2 // i hate losing poets* 62
	o.	*repetitions // phir se* 63
	p.	*ex friends and metaphors* 64
	q.	*more than friends, less than lovers* 65
	r.	*'we were barely friends'* 66
	s.	*now we're back to may* 67

5 purple 69
v. introduction 70

	a.	*purple* 70
	b.	*guessing wishes* 72
	c.	*fate, stars and everything in between* 73
	d.	*ten thirty pm on a school night* 74
	e.	*journals* 75
	f.	*what wounds?* 76
	g.	*colours at thirteen* 77
	h.	*what's with the monsoon and a longing thrill?* 78
	i.	*dreamer* 79
	j.	*travellers* 80
	k.	*car ghosts* 81

- l. *goodbye? a dark hour every night*............ 82
- m. *midnight musings*.. 83

6   **magenta**.. **84**
vi.   introduction.. 85

- a. *meaningless phrase*................................ 85
- b. *withering*.. 86
- c. *you don't deserve poetry so here's just a line*.. 87
- d. *that sums us up nice doesn't it?*............... 88
- e. *unnoticed till it was too late*..................... 89
- f. *the tragedy before december moored*....... 90
- g. *call me a b-grade shakespeare the way i romanticize tragedy*................................. 91
- h. *call me a b-grade shakespeare the way i romanticize tragedy pt.2*.......................... 92
- i. *anatomy*.. 93
- j. *but math was never our strongest suit // geometry 401*... 95
- k. *figuring people out*.................................. 96
- l. *2am and i'm cursing your name*.............. 97
- m. *it's long gone*... 98
- n. *your address is etched in my memory*..... 99
- o. *february birthdays*................................. 100

p.	cpr	101
q.	choices	102
r.	wiser and yet foolish nonetheless	103
s.	forced friendships	104

7   yellow [derogatory] 105
vii.   introduction 106

a.	twelve	106
b.	you're turning this garden barren	107
c.	brutus	108
d.	long cons and moving on	109
e.	the good, bad and ugly	110
f.	wishing well	111
g.	the driftwood didn't save me	112
h.	midnights bleed into afternoons of girl rot	113
i.	jar of hearts	114
j.	validation?	115
k.	how do you get to paradise?	116
l.	architecture	117
m.	love or the lack thereof	118
n.	pinterest quote-esque (pov at eleven)	119
o.	stars (my pov at twelve)	120

	p.	salthouse (pov at thirteen) 121
	q.	heart on her sleeve // advice to pisces? . 122
	r.	roman holiday 123

8 yellow [daisy dove positivity] 124
viii. introduction 125

	a.	life is good 125
	b.	art and the artist 126
	c.	finding hope 127
	d.	lanterns and candles 128
	e.	delicate replicas 129
	f.	unlearning self hate 130
	g.	new beginnings 131

9 the summer i turned pretty 132
ix. introduction 133

	a.	i hate your birthday as much as i hate mine 133
	b.	karmic verse 134
	c.	vision board summer '23 135
	d.	affirmations 136
	e.	when calm had a colour 137
	f.	pastel journals of visions 139
	g.	beige or blue? 140

	h.	did you dream this dream too?	141
	i.	acceptance	142

10 clementines 143
x. introduction 144

	a.	maybe it isn't such a bad thing, really.	145
	b.	mothers and daughters	145
	c.	perhaps she can fix me back	146
	d.	love and loss	147
	e.	sisters	148
	f.	sisters pt. 2	149
	g.	no longer running from ruins?	150
	h.	30.01.23	151
	i.	highkey guide to hurting	152
	j.	lowkey guide to healing?	153
	k.	notions	154
	l.	february spotlight	155
	m.	you are what you leave behind	156
	n.	the scent of goodbye	157
	o.	patterns	158
	p.	once upon a morning	159

11 acknowledgements! 160
12 about the author 162

Anatomy of Letters Unsent

*tuesday tests
and class of '23 core*

introduction

i tiptoe down the stairs.
the wind is breezy
and i'm never late to the bus stop,
 7:05 on the dot.

i eat a full breakfast,
have time to pray,
and counter my grandmother with childish rebuke
for trying to get me into yoga.

poster child, perfect world.
i love to smile, i'm just a girl.

now i curse the elevator for taking a little too long,
hum myself a theme song as i
run with half dried hair
falling into my face.

i haven't eaten anything of substance in the last 16 hours,
but hey! i learnt last night about the law of demand and mickey mouse.
i go to the same school but at a different campus with different people,

the yellow bus that picks me up is a constant;
that's alarming.

the new york and dublin portal opened last week
and that's how i feel,
when i board the bus at 7:15
my childhood has long been set free.

— *my favourite mode of transport is memories*

my final year at [redacted] i sat by the window,
tuesday sharp at 9am, i'd look out of the class,
with the relief of finishing yet another test.
out by the ground, lay the mocking trees; bark shrivelled by winter.
leaves' anarchic scream, Stalingrad over spring
but one tuesday, 9:10.
for the first time i noticed a tree in full bloom.
amidst the autumn flowers i'd seen before,
names i hadn't bothered to learn

// i think back to childhood, freshly cut grass
i was barely three, side door to the balcony
things i thought i'd quite forgotten.
my best friend on the stage,
my mother in the crowd,
nightshade crept slowly,
freshly cut grass //

the same tree in the garden by the graveyard,
seventh grade on an ipod
i tried to capture a shot.
nineteen, i felt smaller than before
i wondered how i left the shore

— *mid examination epiphanies*

an era too short, a destruction too long,
i had a friend, a foe and a million little woes.

when i looked at you, i found a home;
words in margins,
pages of memories,
yellow, orange, brown, beige,
fever blues in the bus bay.

so long; au revoir

i looked at you and found a home
now i'm afraid to be alone.

— *class of '23*

10am on a saturday morning,
quite possible the last time
i see the smile on your face as
someone calls your name.

the way you hang your sweater,
the way you sign yearbooks,
the curve of your hand over the railing,
the curl in your hair, subject to the wind.

everything, everything, everything.
a decade full of longing, falling, crashing.
everything, everything, everything
how is it goodbye isn't this supposed to be the beginning?

— *midsummer march*

i want your cardigan to
engulf me;

scent of fury,
rain and agony.
i want the next 191 days,
solitude and secrets,
every breathing moment till goodbye,
the raindrops silent.

after tonight,
we never meet;
we make promises to
but we never actually do.

and i'll remember –
every fight,
every laugh,
every glance,
every touch,
every picture,
every memory,
every goodbye.
– the tragedy of a starless night

— *shakespearean vows*

i used to scoff at people my age telling me about childhood friends as if they were flickering fragments of an obscure past.

that's because i had my "people" in every memory i secured within.

i had lunch with the same people five days a week, forty two weeks and year and twelve years so.

oh but how we push the chairs into the desks, pack our bags and switch the lights off on our way out.

and we'll carve new lives,
from new places and new people,
and come back once in three years,
when we'll rush and meet,
take pictures and leave (again)

forgetting – to reminisce how i can't make coffee and about S's mom's spicy potato curry and how everyone hates J and her mom but continue to suck up to them

forlorn,
disastrous,
disheartening.

how all i wished for was to wander –
to fly and hope and dream and live (leave)
but now i wish to be stuck in this moment,
a time loop for eternity,
because to wander now,
is to walk away in ways,
in ways, you cannot control.

— *to live is to leave*

all these years,
i've been held by the same people,
good, bad, ugly, love, hate.
the same people.

but now,
the cascading ocean catches up;
i tumble across waves,
tread across the wind,
and for the first time,

i want the fights and the screams
and the tiresome back.

i want the familiarity back,

i want the things i've willingly left
i need it back to hold my hand.
i need a time-loop standstill and frozen
dear childhood, i feel alone

— *dear childhood*

death by a thousand cuts

introduction

this is the beginning of my indirect love letters to travel,
it's about when i'm twenty-six and backpacking through a city i can't wait to unravel.

it's about my future with all of its glory and sadness, mostly nostalgic because there's no other way i'd have it.

it's probably just my version of wannabe adulthood undone. (but also)
it's about all the love lost and all the life earned, it's about my daydreams and lessons learnt,
my girls who i gave it all to, but they never called in return.

this chapter is an exploration of themes i've envisioned in a particular hue
heavily influenced by a song i had on repeat for a majority of 2022
subtle pinks and charming blues

— *flashbacks from my future waking me up*

i.

you walk home on a friday night with a bag full of paperwork and a carton full of headache. the music coursing through your ears has been on repeat for the last twenty three minutes and you haven't noticed. songs you used to dance to, now make you break down and block your ways to breathe. in a city full of dreams, how do you dream without sleep?

ii.

the light in the house stopped working two months ago. you never noticed because you're almost never home. the study is illuminated by the glow of the Korean convenience store across the

street. your house is a mess; your wardrobe has no birthday dress. the kitchen hasn't been touched since the day you moved in. your walls have inspirational quotes you absolutely don't believe in.

iii.

your friends meet at a pub on the West End and dance on the High Line till midnight. they called and called until trust and memories faded to be replaced by lines etched by distance. friday nights involve avoiding phone calls from home; whatever that is.

iv.

the ice cream expired last night. you take medicine for headache and eat halloween candy from last year. yesterday you were sixteen, now suddenly you've aged a decade.

// in my head i do everything right //

— *untitled.mp4 (2022)*

the inner rounds of the walk track
are more intimate,
there's not much activity,
and i can pretend that i'm in the alleyway
home to the overpriced apartment,
i work hard and afford at some point in my twenties;

my twenties,
when all this tragedy
has the courage to transform into poetic value.

twenties —
where i get my final chance to fall in love hard enough
to freeze time and write back
to dozens of letters i've sent myself;
the practical equivalent of coming back to hold my hand
in the alleyways i pretend lead to my twenties

— *adulting fantasies*

i.
mosaic fires
break my holy ground,
saturn tried to
heal me from above.

ii.
king of clubs, queen of spades,
the things i don't understand.
call me a devil, call me babe
burgundy quicksand.

iii.
city full of murals,
in a postcard in the corner,
my body is a ghost,
my mind is an illusion
people don't remember.
no matter how alluring
my voice sounds too foreign
am i beloved or am i forgotten?

— *call me by my name*

days bring months,
the leaves call or drop by once
in a while,
yet your letter never arrives.

— *you're an equation i can never derive*

you put a letter on my windshield,
three days before i left,
running through this city,
figuring out footsteps.
you wanted things that couldn't be kept,
the last of what was left.
burning in embers,
halfway across the globe,
falling tears in september,
fingerprints on my soul.

— *tales from my worn out honda city*

i have this picture of us,
eight months from now,
when we graduate;
our eyes meet,
from across the stage.
and
i'll hear lorde in the background,
i'll say it could've been different,
i'll see you nodding in unison,
i'll fall back into you again.
or
we'll stay where we are,
we'll trace our line of art,
we'll smile and let it pass,
we'll reminisce falling apart.

— *grad*

how i wish,
we kept the promises
we made at six,
till we were sixteen.

— *old friends after summer died blue*

you choose grieving hues for my portrait,
and all of my eulogies exhilarate you .

you once traced my face till my chin dipped into moonlight,
tucked my hair back till my sadness falls out of place.

i wake up now to anonymous messages in my inbox, hoping each one bears your name; i was convinced i forgot.

what happened to those summers you promised us,
the field green as we discussed life and love.

try to inject amnesia,
longing, angst, dismissal, fever weak.

it was a midsummer night,
but it wasn't a dream.

— *to may, we were bestfriends*

i don't like eternal spring,
it reminds me of you,
and broken heart galleries
filled with inexorable,
and unfathomable déjà vu.

— *i don't like eternal spring*

sometimes denial feels real,
like i'm no longer thinking of you.

but every now and then, i keep meeting someone new,
as if all of us has run its course.
this town is red,
remember when we painted it blue?

— *letting go but staying true*

once a priority, now settled in the end of the call list
the cafe in the corner,
has a picture on the wall,
of our evenings over there,
and mornings on the sidewalk.

i clutch my fist,
trying, to hold on to this,
but it drifts away;

the last ember of our thin wafting smoke,
lost in the sea of all the things i once used to hold.

— *slipping away*

(if i could tell you how much i loved you trust me i would)

you're out with your friends,
wearing my necklace;

you were laughing about something,
it brought out your freckles

your hair out of place,
i remember the last days

pretending i was forever;
my name means nothing anymore.

arguments with others,
when i know you're not worth fighting for.

struggling to breathe,
when you can strike a fire and walk free,
lying through your bare teeth.

farewell until next time,
i hope we never meet.

(if i could tell you how much i hate you trust me i would)

— *scream queens*

what if i'm 31,
satisfied with my life,
duvet wrapped around me,
on the couch on a friday night.

but my friends go out without me
and suddenly i'm fifteen,
my face itching where my tears dry,
except this time i did everything right,
only to find it was all a lie.

— *rational (until proven irrational) fears*

Anvita Bhogadi

midnight swim

introduction

in my makeshift marsh,
i let moments soar,
in post rain petrichor.

the water is blue,
moonlight anew,
it's time again to pick at my wounds.

— *therapy from a swim session*

skinny dipping at midnight,
her name a whisper in the water.
half asleep at daylight,
it's her again, even louder.
by the fire in the kitchen,
the bed, the bath and the living.
the song on the radio,
the dust on the piano,
my fingertips;
it still stings,
every bit of me,
covered by her name,
from this half forgotten dream.

— *ancestral visions*

my love was like the plants we brought,
growing though i stopped watering–

// hands imprinted on the windows,
lilacs over the bathtub,
magazines untouched in the corridor,
the perfume i loved,
half finished paintings,
half eaten desserts. //

— *two lilacs in the corner slowly growing apart*

— *two lilacs*

dreaming in the city lights,
her portrait by the simmering fire,
her smile– an august landscape,
her eyes – a haunting daze.

dreaming in the city lights,
said she was here to stay,
instead she left me with plenty to erase.

— *hey, remember our concrete jungle filled with dreams?*

i sit by the vatican night,
they still haven't fixed the tubelight
in half the places we used to sneak around,
i try to feel what i could've if we
let our guards down.

i let our sorrow be my story,
still i have the same dream.
sweet summer child; twenty three,
wash my shore i'll be floating free.

— *vatican night*

three months ago,
you told me you never loved me
because you need to like me to begin with.
so was this friendship just a mirage?
or is it a truth that feels too much?
to carry, the lies
of your new life.

— *she taught me women can be cruel too*

to this day i wonder;
i made you my mural,
i made you my muse.
were we just friends,
or lovers confused?

— *tumblr girls (2021) // art museum thoughts*

they ask me about a friend i haven't spoken to in months. i feel the chill in my bones when i recount words last said; the hurt, the annoyance and the betrayal.

they ask me now of people i used to love and watch me stutter trying to hold back all emotion. the rawest way of saying i miss you is never doing it.

— *my entire personality is just longing for old friends and forgive but not forget*

all my friends are yours now,
they put you on the pedestal.
bruises back on burnt ground,
i guess we mess things up well.
all your friends are mine too,
what's up with this anti-climatic ruse?
is this feeling screaming blue?
slow-burn silent short circuit.

— *sides*

the sounds die in her throat —
her mother's laughter,
her father's banter,
her garden of thorns,
glimmering hope gone.

the sand at the beach,
the apple orchard and the fallen peach,
fingers clasped together,
moments now locked up,

— *the keys submerged as the water consumed*

— *one evening with the waves*

when nightfall dances with moonlight,
and stars descend into heavens,
flickering beams of yellow strike,
the dreamer's heart, no longer alone.

music hit the vine,
sleep slumped by the bedside,
feet on the floor,
in a world of their own,
head filled with electric hearts.

— *once upon a midnight spark*

i have a secret to tell,
said the moon,
that raven-hair girl; she's in love with you.
i closed my eyes and looked at hues;
i can't bear it if it isn't true,
because raven-hair girl,
i'm in love with you.

— *secrets of the moon*

cold end of the pool,
i jumped right in.
dark secret; keep revisiting,
sweet talks, trust falls, clandestine harmony.
asphalt by the cliffside,
should've fled at the first signs.
the memory that keeps threatening,
was way better off as a fleeting feeling.

— *garden of time*

when she was five,
she wondered about the lake outside.
were there swans and seagulls?
a world full of water?
leaf, branch, twig, leaf
she lay looking at her tapestry.
a forest in its own right,
a vine of decoration // her mother's sole belonging
when she was fifteen,
she knew there was no lake outside,
seagulls and swans and extinct lives,
water eviscerated into cloud hives.
words on a wall,
civilizations fell apart,
paint peeling stray, a world fading away,
 leaf, branch, twig, leaf

— *one of the last remaining*

i
starlight, i felt nothing.
i saw complete auroras,
light — peaking, beaming, surrendering,
amalgamation of auras.

ii.
moonshine i'm left hollow,
bruising myself for words.
i wish they were immaculate as before,
tired lightly — double edged sword.

iii.
clouds long for me to spill,
there is ache and longing,
yet no splattered ink.

— *the night sky didn't help me write (writer's block in a midnight age)*

ivy grew,
where my field of daisies bloomed,
picking apart every petal,
locking in; its cages of metal.

air tight when the moss trickled in,
pierced it from within,
so close, yet so different,
i try to reach you when i can't sleep,
my mind is a shrine i forget to clean,
now you're always in my periphery.

— *my sleep cycle's as messed as you*

Anatomy of Letters Unsent

5:43PM

introduction

it's like
when you paint a sky,
and you have only three go-to colours.

so you dip the whole thing,
in purple, blue and pink.

the shades make no difference,
my confusion still prevails,
my decisiveness is quite blind,
do i kiss you, kill you, or lose my mind?

— *sunsets in a modern age*

seagulls at the riverside,
magnolias under withering winter eyes.

i've heard this song before,
i try to heal but it doesn't work.

my psyche to scared to see,
the white flames my eyes reek.

the leaves in motion abruptly stop,
to shower their pity on broken stars.

what use is passing sympathy,
with no knowledge of the backstory.

i walked this road a million times,
in each of my forgotten lives.

we've been here before the mind cries,
all i remember is déjà vu flying by.

— *lavender blossoms*

if it's all part
of a dream
will it hurt
any less?

— *my subconscious lingers for way too long*

is it weird that
i return to your muse
everytime i'm out of ideas.

how i go over every word,
every laugh,
every inside joke,
every moment of yours,
just to search for something,
i haven't yet driven myself crazy over

if closure was effective,
i'd have a million new beginnings.
maybe i'm delusional,
maybe there is no ending to us.

— *writer's block*

we kiss
(the snow/ it melts / the sparks / they disperse)
we watch the sunset
(the red / it's gone / the blue / it's cruel)
you bring me ice-cream
(it's pistachio / you know / i hate it)
i pick the movie
(it's a comedy / i know / you won't enjoy it)
you left the stove on
(in the kitchen / how the flames dance / instead of us)
now we don't walk
(in crowds)
when the angels (above us)
leak tears watching us
(falling out of love)

— *falling out of love*

my thumb shakes
when i touch your face
(i still love you)
your eyes search for mine in crowds
(i still love you)
your fingers reach for mine
and don't let go
(i still love you)
your lips touch my wrist
my pulse is swift
(i still love you)
your hands wrapped
around her waist

— *i still love you*

we were born dreamers;
it's only fitting
that we live so

— *405*

i don't know
anything anymore

my body is a chore
my mind years to soar
my heart is in a piece
of long lost folklore

— *beach read*

I
i like to belong
to hotel hallways and airports;
belong to things with a certain allure
but not in a glitzy glamorous way,
it's more like
a lonely, homesick way.

II
the planes connect my future and present
the dim rooms cradle my past

III
the wind carries me everywhere but home
the heavy covers guarantee me escape
but what if i choose to ignore everything
and go back?
but i don't
sometimes, it's better to be alone
than face some remnants

— *home away from home?*

august passes by
yet again i have a hard time adjusting.
regrets of not having enjoyed it.
haunted by how i have to wait nine months to live again.

oh! to imagine how many summers,
how many winter and autumns
faded into dust, how many wandered away,
unlived to my full capacity.

how many beach runs i've missed.
how many crumpled leaves never fell as i danced in the middle of the road.
how many misty midnights i had poisoned toast.

the caterpillar turned into a butterfly and a failure into i
a sweet young girl full of mischief, now a teenager laden with grief.

— *august slipped away*

i.

last september

i sat by the

material to be perused

"when connected in parallel; a voltmeter

when connected in series; an ammeter"

i sat there watching hours die

night after night

wishing to be freed

from this ungodly urge to sit by–

the showers, breathe in the petrichor

fall out with the sun and

tune myself to the music of the world

ii.

this april, i sit by the

now scattered leaves on a skinny stick

what once was spring bloom; now autumn laden

no material in front of me

no physics to study

no plan, no strategy

no path seems correct

the future violently bleak

freedom;

are you truly liberating?

— *september tears and april fears*

the leaves keep changing colours,
i keep screaming at others.

everything is just a replication of all we never had,
we run behind people we know we'll never catch.

the things we love always fall apart,
the heart goes on, but the circle comes back to the start.

— *looped*

whimsical october colors
and secluded lanes,

the illicit affair between
sunshine and window panes,

leaves down your wall
waiting for winter's kiss,

lend me the cloth to clean my spectacles,
don't let this be an upended miracle.

picture frames right in place,
wilder laughs; forget our grace,

fingers to interlace with,
a warmer time's feeble dream,

can we cue
the indie music?

— *only in october*

november is [**] scary
because what if i
slip into seasonal depression
for three minutes

and suddenly
the only person i can talk to
is my ghost

and there's a new group chat
of the people i love the most
deciding whether or not
i'm worth loving

— *it doesn't matter anymore but back then it really did*

all of the hurt in my life
was already taught to me
by twin mirrored souls
just like yours;
all of you
now relieves me.

so when i,
take a walk around the park,
or enter a door they left ajar,
i stop to grieve and repeat;

all my friends from home,
might've left me alone,
but i'm not troubled to breathe.

because all of the hurt in my life,
was already taught to me
by twin mirrored souls
just like yours;
all of you
now relieves me.

— *circle moment*

they speak of moving on from relationships
but it doesn't work for us does it?
we, were the same, yet different
bound to grieve over something
we can never truly understand

— *grieving friendships*

birch branches covered in snow,
faces basking in glow,
hands moved the way
we made magic with our words,
i wonder how you articulate
the feelings snatched away,
when you thought they could last
a lifetime.

— grieving friendships pt. 2 // i hate losing poets

i know i promised,
but if you really meant it,
i would still let you in,
forgetting you would break me, again

— *repetitions // phir se*

ashes were a pyre's remains,
a puddle was the rain's,
a cocoon is the caterpillar's,
just like the ruins of my heart.
are still covered by traces of my girls.

— *ex friends and metaphors*

my hand reaches for yours,
knowing you'll pull away,
our laughs tangled in lore,
maybe this isn't the game to play.

what it was in the beginning,
it will never be.
falling back, diving thrice,
if only you could see.

dream a little dream of me,
we're dancing down the willow creek,
your hand pulls away from me,
not knowing i truly mean it.

— *more than friends, less than lovers*

when i'd tell you all my deepest
darkest fears,
and you'd reassure me,

everything will be alright,
when your hand,
held onto mine,

as we turned the math
textbook to page no. 149

pick me as the partner,
in all your science projects,
proofread my speeches,
before debate contests.

your sister's favourite colour,
etched in my mind,
best friends,
yet you never said it.

— *'we were barely friends'*

we don't know who we are anymore,
mid july, there's no light
are we at the shore?

not long ago
i remember someone wrote,
we should talk more,
i wonder where did that go?

i let the momentum fall,
let new signs call,
try to stay,
but walk away all the same

pointed flame,
perspective's to blame
tell me now,
are we okay?

— *now we're back to may*

turquoise skies lavender lies
walk down the mosaic path

but now i'm lost in the arcade
of a broken heart

   — *arcadia*

Anatomy of Letters Unsent

purple

introduction

she sits slowly digging down the rabbit hole
she knows she shouldn't.

oh memory within the eye!
i've manipulated you, haven't i?

which wound do we pick now?
how long till this wears off?

she unravels her boxed regret;
it's time to play trauma roulette

— *purple*

i thought i could never write again,
that perhaps i was a
zero point five hit wonder.

but how foolish was i to think,
or perhaps not think enough.

because one dead summer ,
does not mean a graveyard of all i can be,
maybe i need a moment to myself,
before i heal and break and heal.

my nerves are crisp,
the weather up here is amiss, hold myself or fall apart,
i do it all again for art.

— *comeback?*

if i could wish, i think i would.
but in a stream of glass,
silent worlds that dance,
where roads keep converging,
and people keep colliding,

in midst of an obituary of war,
who am i to ignore what the soul wants?

but when the heart reaches for,
a dream better left untouched,
i could wish, but i wouldn't.

— *guessing wishes*

i left the stars for the sea,
(secrets on my feet)

left my home for a dream
(a dream i don't believe)

rolled the dice on my future,
(miracles and illusions)

i left the stars for the sea,
(so they took everything from me)

— *fate, stars and everything in between*

she lay there,
screen flickering,
notes scattered,
ink on paper,
candles on the wall
she lay there,
hair on her face,
light in the corner,
colours fading
she lay there,
tired, numb and hoping;
longing for childhood.

— *ten thirty pm on a school night*

scrawny writing in my journals –
supposedly making me reflect
but really all it does
is make me feel depressed

— *journals*

cut me up
tear me down

all you find

are the moments
and memories.

— *what wounds?*

lavenders; crystal dew glint,
a calming sense in a heated sprint.

the touch of blue,
in chromatic screams,
weaves enigmatic tales,
with captivating seams.

the intricacies keep returning like a half-forgotten dream.
how i hope these tangled myriad feelings never leave.

my body protests sleep,
my mind yearns for peace.

— *colours at thirteen*

a random memory.
a triggered domino effect,
leading to some sort of epiphany,
the false sense of security when time stands still.

— *what's with the monsoon and a longing thrill?*

i just wish i can be happy in the future.
(it's too tiring in here)

— *dreamer*

we're travellers;
trying to find a whole lot of everything,
and realizing that the answers lie at home.

— *travellers*

i carry ghosts in the car trunk,
of all the people i used to be —
a girl breathing alone,
a girl in an orange sundress,
a girl who fought,
a girl who fell,
a little too short but survived,
a girl with too many goodbyes

i carry ghosts in the car trunk,
all dragged down by the moments where i'm stuck.

— *car ghosts*

non-existent normality
wishing it never ends; nocturnity
is this hell by decisions or design?
can i get hurrah for the last ride?

the back and forth of visions in my crumbling mind
mumbling about a future that never was
isn't there something i can try?
maybe some stronger adrenaline rush?

i think my heart is sweating
burnt out from trying
to love the ones i thought were mine.

time? unreal.
life? overrated.
trust? a forgotten vice.
goodbye? a dark hour every night.

— *goodbye? a dark hour every night.*

by the grave i saw the sorrows;
the acedia in my heart,
i ponder if i shall see the morrow,
or watch myself break apart.

— *midnight musings*

Anvita Bhogadi

magenta

introduction

i've rewritten myself as many times as it took me,
to erase the seared image of my happiness when i was nine.
(i'd keep it around, but i'm no longer doing life right)

i've been gatsby for my women —
friends forever was always their favourite line,
yet i'll still fall if you ask me one more time.

i write to scream, cut the whispers and chase,
but everyone wants only two lines when i have a paragraph to say.

here's my worst poetry,

— *meaningless phrase*

winter isn't really something specific,
it's loosely based nostalgia.
maybe something more
but on some nights,
that's all the burden
you can take on.

— *withering*

i heard my heartbeat today.
it was screaming
your name.

— you don't deserve poetry so here's just a line

the title's longer than the story

— *that sums us up nice doesn't it?*

you crept into my heart
like winter crept into november.

— *unnoticed till it was too late*

if you were a season,
you would fall between
june and november.
a little sunshine,
a little hail
a little loss.

the spring of june,
the winter of august,
the fall of november.

you'd be the glass in the sawdust woods, the tales from the meadow's hood.
the water in the rustling brook.
the tragedy before december moored.

— *the tragedy before december moored*

what if i told you,
we were meant to be,
but we couldn't
because it's always a tragedy,
to love someone,
you never knew entirely

— *call me a b-grade shakespeare the way i romanticize tragedy*

what a shame
that all the games
had to end now;
we were poetry
trapped in the tragedy
of life.

— *call me a b-grade shakespeare the way i romanticize tragedy pt.2*

an agonized heart doesn't not know quiet,
tears of my mind reach my lips,
like the blood on the edge of my fingertips.
the words in my lungs go numb on my tongue,
the blood in my veins is as rusty as us.

my eyes speak volumes you cannot hear,
you can't see my arms struggling with the want to bring you near,
you can't read my face
spiralling down the staircase;
what a cliche screaming stay.

— *anatomy*

anemoia
// noun //

1. nostalgic about things you've never experienced before
2. you and i

we are parallel lines,
travelling through time,
hoping that one day,
a diversion stumbles our way
to bring us together.

— *but math was never our strongest suit //*
   geometry 401

your name tastes less foreign now,
words less haunting.
we were 'wrong person wrong time'
but with the right story.
time will teach other tales,
but this is the one i hold closest to me.

— *figuring people out*

he keeps writing me letters on parchment,
annotates my books with his heart and
holds my hand but it feels like a lot (more)

but time and time again,
i think about fingers brushing,
mistakes in making.

it's been long overdue,
nothing feels right,
the way i loved you
is still on my mind.

he keeps writing me letters on parchment,
yet it isn't where my heart is

— *2am and i'm cursing your name*

your brown leather jacket,
my hair in my face.
stopped the car midway,
looking at the foliage.

should've known it; down the road
the leaves were falling apart
you used to carry groceries
now i'm pushing a broken cart.

looking out the window,
you were looking at me.
now it's winter with a coarse glow
you aren't calling back for me.

— *it's long gone*

up in the clouds,
i remember seeing you.
but what work does the demon do
in an angel's abode?

— *your address is etched in my memory*

your birthday is five days later,
and i have your number this time. but i can't call or message you, because this time around,
we're strangers.

— *february birthdays*

my heart's in my lungs;
it's stuck-
now i can't breathe
without feeling your presence.

— *cpr*

i can feel the waves
the magnetism,
the helplessness.

it started with words
ended with tangles.

clandestine exchanges at midnight
shameful greetings in daylight.

pretending to not know all the,
thoughts we poured out hours ago.

in the deep waters, out of time
the question remains: can we let go?

— *choices*

we were a cautionary tale,
for people rushing into fate
how wise of me to not take
my own advice
and collide with something else.

— *wiser and yet foolish nonetheless*

only when i said it out loud,
did i understand that it was absurd,
how can i possibly miss you so much
when we were never even close.

— *forced friendships*

yellow [derogatory]

introduction

i was twelve,
and i wrote bad poetry
about wanting to be sixteen.

as if a change in the number on my cake,
meant i'd miraculously become happier, shinier and worthier
of whatever dreams i spent my childhood chasing.

dreams so concrete, yet i cannot recollect them now; i've passed through too many personalities
than anyone should be allowed.

now i'm sixteen and i haven't written in two years oh how i desperately crave to be twelve.

— *twelve*

cadence of the morrow,
tinted by your sorrow,
spring in the meadow,
shadow beside me
dark and alone.

everytime i let you out,
a silent whisper; you creep back in.

please spare my heart of this
sulking, ruining, running.

— *you're turning this garden barren*

i thought i was too cursed
and bruised
to fly.

my wings cut
and my hopes burnt
i guess you were
the devil all the time.

— *brutus*

kaleidoscope of fragmented memories
that are dancing in the shadows
but not in front of me,
your rusting letters
right where you left me.

the collision is real strong,
when i'm stuck in the storm
the red flags are misted,
no wonder i missed them.

we could stay here for ages,
but it's called a breaking point for a reason.
what a failure of a long con,
here's to moving on.

— *long cons and moving on*

smiles hide
devious lies,
gnarls try to deny
torturous passing of time,
freckles try to imply
beauty isn't finite.

the good are just bad ones
who've never been caught.

the bad are just good ones
who've put up with a lot.

the ugly are just pretty ones
filled with distraught.

— *the good, bad and ugly*

we're all barely wading
through waters of solitude,
translucent cages of cruelty,
laced with insincere apologies
of the people we believed in naively.

but now, we're trapped,
in a spiralling stairwell
descending us into misery
and then hell.

— *wishing well*

the driftwood didn't save me;
it kept me afloat
long enough
to give me hope
and drown me.

— *the driftwood didn't save me*

inhabitant of my head,
spiral of shame,
feeling unsafe out of bed,
pondering is a treacherous game.

— *midnights bleed into afternoons of girl rot*

break a heart
leave a scar
break another.
i've got a jar of hearts
burning for the sole purpose
of loving you.

— *jar of hearts*

i write letters to people, knowing they won't be read,
i write poetry knowing i won't be appreciated
i loathe the person who said ignorance is bliss;
i'd rather be dead than be ignored like this

— *validation?*

i want large waterfalls,
woodlands mystic and tall,
artifact garden,
pseudo sky lanterns.

but how do you get to paradise
from the lowest rung of the darkest depths?
how do you love a sunrise
when despair is all you have left?

— *how do you get to paradise?*

it seems like something
has broken from its seams. no,
not my bone
no not my home
oh! i've broken my dreams.

— *architecture*

i have been writing
about heart break since i was twelve.
why? because that is so much more easier to confront than friend breakups and social disconnection.

— *love or the lack thereof*

they say aim for the moon
you'll fall on the stars
but what if you float through space
adorned with scars.

— *pinterest quote-esque (pov at eleven)*

when i was a kid
i tried writing about stars
but there was always quite something i couldn't capture.

maybe it is because
stars are too broken
trying to light up our lives
that they didn't want to be written about.

because it would mean
breaking is beautiful on the outside,
and people would want to break themselves
for people who wouldn't even notice,
the way stars break themselves for us.

— *stars (my pov at twelve)*

the salthouse looked over the storms and the clouds
and the seas.
the salthouse saw the people
and the sunsets and the families.
it saw the skies cry, the oceans dry
and the horizon burn.
the salthouse saw them build lives
in front of it, behind it
around it and over it.

but who looked at the salthouse?
no one.

— *salthouse (pov at thirteen)*

to the girl who trusts
everyone when they call her beautiful:
darling they called rome beautiful,
doesn't mean they stayed
when it started to burn.

— *heart on her sleeve // advice to pisces?*

what if they're the dreamy ocean,
what if they're the sun.
do you want to drown?
do you want to burn?

— *roman holiday*

Anvita Bhogadi

yellow [daisy dove positivity]

introduction

this ending doesn't sting
it doesn't pierce me apart;
the way i thought it would

it calms me,
relieves me,
satisfies me.

— *life is good*

after i got my closure,
(my pain healed, my body sane
my mind more alive than it had ever been)

i couldn't stop writing:
hurt, floating ending, breathing;
beginnings.

it was never you that fuelled me to write,
inspired yes, but you were not my being.

all this while i thought not having you stunted me,
but it turned out to be the completely accepted lack of
you that helped me grow.

i will never again insult my art
for you; ever
i promise this
i owe this
to myself.

— *art and the artist*

the thing about grief is,
you expect it to pass
somehow all it ever does is grow.

but one day,
the rain looks brighter,
the chill feels warmer,
and the dark seams – escapable.

— *finding hope*

little miss sunshine
lit up a thousand lives.
but she never realized
she could've lit up the darkness inside.

— *lanterns and candles*

humans are not butterflies
so why do we try too hard
to be exactly
like someone else?

— *delicate replicas*

it's okay to love someone passionately
with butterflies in your stomach
and sparks on your fingertips.

it's okay to love someone so hard
that you eradicate their insecurities.

it's okay if that someone is you.

— *unlearning self hate*

where one friendship ends there begins another.
so this is me, falling back in love
with the whole wide world
all the good, bad, ugly and the hate.

— *new beginnings*

Anvita Bhogadi

the summer i turned pretty

introduction

tales from a city i'm afraid to revisit,
dreams from the pictures i'm scared to open.
folders i haven't unlocked in two years,
my trauma-versary snaps into place every other month.
did we have to celebrate life so much?

— *i hate your birthday as much as i hate mine*

we let the moments stay,
impulses calling our names,
sapphires in our visions,
fallen secret liaisons,
wind in my hair,
sucked out from the space
between us,
Holidays.

— *karmic verse*

scheming too thick,
scarlet meadow,
pearls around our neck,
oceanic pretext.
three books on the towel,
sand in my hair,
you're crying to your mother
we've been walking fine lines too long,
following dead trails too far.
searching for a home in the summer,
sixteen isn't enough.
may 13,
we drove down to the beach,
suburbia's asleep.
the radio's blasting;
imperial silence.

— *vision board summer '23*

if i had another chance,
i'd let things stay the same,
because and eternity
of promised nothings,
is better than the
hope of 'one day'

— *affirmations*

the blue could've been violence,
the blue could've been sad,
the blue could've been alarming
but i chose it for my silence,
and the heart that relaxed.

— *when calm had a colour*

we dip our feet
in cerulean seas.

we gorge the clementines
and dig our nails into the remaining.

we write our names in the sand
and dance around the winds; wild.

we hold hands
and run as if we're on our last ride.

(we pull the grass off the land/
we only thrive in tartare hues)

we tear open spring
for a mint beach drink.

bleak winters;
but we pull out autumn from golden afternoons.

this year, we choose summer –
chromium sunlight over heartbreak blue.

we choose freedom over captivity;
choose life and colour
we choose happiness
we choose memories.

— *pastel journals of visions*

"beige or blue?"

>car wreck on the side road
>heartbeat in a wild code
>summer setting in the dark
>your mother's begging you to call.

>car wreck on the side road
>heartbeat now a morse code
>pardon me, i'll cry
>and then you can choose.

beige or blue?

— *beige or blue?*

last night i dreamt we talked again
in the aftermath we settled right in;
that two years of betrayal and agony,
extinguish to pave way for confessions and new beginnings

last night i dreamt we talked again,
but a dream is a dream
and that's how it remains.

— *did you dream this dream too?*

but it isn't as painful,
as i expect it to be,
time in generous,
our minds pertinent,
maybe the after effects are over
maybe i'm still in love,
how ever that works
i guess when you crash into the sea,
you burn before you're free.

— *acceptance*

clementines

introduction

can you peel my oranges for me?

i've spent so long trying not to be my mother,
that i led myself to that very destiny —
the way i swapped coffee for chamomile
the way i looked for happy ending in sad stories
the way petrichor trumped the smell of petrol
the way i fought and fought and survived – every time

— *maybe it isn't such a bad thing, really.*

— *mothers and daughters*

and sometimes
everything gets
a little too heavy and
all i wish for
is my mother.

— *perhaps she can fix me back*

yesterday i dreamt of a sunflower field
where my mother sat down
and braided my hair.

today i saw a sunflower and wept,
for all of the space between us
and the words unsaid.

— *love and loss*

i want to hold her in my arms,
golden blankets woven around,
securing her imminent charm,
my responsibility — my holy ground.

— *sisters*

you are the light of my life,
a star that's burning bright
but that's all you are
just a star with distances i can't cover
and gaps i can't bridge
you are a star
and i can only love you
from afar.

— *sisters pt. 2*

i searched for beauty
far and wide,
but i caught her scent in
scar and smile,
i searched love in an ethereal garden
garnered a couple baffled glances,
i searched for happiness in the "best" places
high society; made a fool of myself.

what's good for others isn't for you
and sometimes the best things
can be unearthed in ruins too.

— *no longer running from ruins?*

a sentence changed my life,
the silence changed it even more,
one text steered me towards hope,
life taught me every answer isn't the truth.

— *30.01.23*

i sit, cry, repeat,
forget to restock the ice cream
i don't sleep for a week
stirring pots
and burning hands (thrice already)
does everybody hate me?
i stalk people on social media,
send them messages at 2:58 am
unfollow old friends,
but ask an acquaintance how they're doing.

— *highkey guide to hurting.*

i grow plants,
delete instagram,
eat ammamma's food,
dance to my favourite song,
drop my sister at the bus stop,
leave the caffeine to my mother,
start learning a new language (failing miserably but it's alright)
little things i started noticing.

— *lowkey guide to healing?*

not all nights have stars
not all traumas have scars
not all love is beautiful
not all goodbyes are cruel.

— *notions*

6am in the february daylight,
i spin around the room in imaginary spotlight,
but this time it's neither madness nor pain.

life, are you calling again?

— *february spotlight*

who are we,
if not the marks we leave behind —
the paint on her fingers.
burnt toast in the kitchen.

the ink on the paper.
the juice on the counter.

one smile at midnight.
a secret at sunrise.

a red dress in the closet.
a hug that feels like sunset.

— *you are what you leave behind*

coffee from a morning that we passed by,
september love mourning all its lies,
calling home but i can't recollect the number,
ashes piling up where there once were embers.

the shirt on the corner rack
screaming but no one to have our back,
a peck on the cheek
in the middle of the night,
you turn off the porch light
on your way outside.

i know it too well,
the scent of goodbye.

— *the scent of goodbye*

human tendency
is to find patterns in every phenomenon.

mine fuel predictions
about how my friendships end.

until the sea taught me
i can be okay.

every wave,
seemed the same.

until they culminated
in a different way

what if all my love
doesn't turn into hate?

what if life,
turns out to be fair?

— *patterns*

the season brought me chill in my bones,
new hands to hold,

blood coursing with pulses
of places i've never been to before,
breath on my skin that feels like home.
— *once upon a morning*

Acknowledgements!

In the time this book has been titled *midnight rose* and rechristened to *orange and other sunsets* to finally where we are today — *the anatomy of letters unsent* — there's only a few people who've been through it all.

Here's to Ammamma and Tatagaru for always believing in me (and so many more things but if I got into that we'd need a whole trilogy). To my mom and dad, thank you for never giving up on trying. To my dearest Naisha, I'll always love you. When you're older and reading this I want you to remember I'll always be there for you no matter what.

To Arunima Ma'am – the first person to open the door of literary possibilities to me and notice that I could write. Thank you for seeing my potential even at the age of seven amidst all those phrases copied from Enid Blyton or the stories ending with "woke up to realize it was a dream".

Here's to Nisha, who's going to laugh at this acknowledgement. You've been my emotional anchor for so long, this section would be incomplete without you in it. Thank you for the midnight rants and the college talks and unfiltered ambitions.

Dear Sumedha, I know we don't acknowledge emotional intimacy but I'm truly proud of who we've become today and I'll always love you. Thanks for trying to grow old with me.

Dear Krishna, thanks for being the best spicy pisces girl to my salty pisces. To more KitKats and finance girl dreams.

To Vania – your goofiness lights up my nights and puzzles my mornings. Our paani puri dates keep me alive.

To Tanmai and Virat — thanks for sticking by. You guys know how much it means.

To Neha — Though you played the most crucial role in shaping the next collection, I can't fathom not thanking you for this one.

To Sanskriti and being girls together — Thank you for making me believe in the power of email catharsis and safe places.

To my readers, I love you for making twelve year old me happy, thirteen year old me confused and fourteen year old me validated by reading and supporting my art.

love, hope and memories
Anvita Bhogadi.

About The Author

anvita bhogadi is a sixteen year old indian poet and writer who romanticizes nostalgia a little too much, which explains her *mahanati* and *la la land* obsession. she has been writing since eight years of age and chasing dreams of publishing since 11, but has been heavily set back by procrastination and cbse board years (read: procrastination).

second daughter to her grandparents, tea-spiller to her mother, wannabe politico to her father and a completely uninteresting and uncool person to her sister – *anvita* is a future award winning author for her poorly plagiarized version of harry potter written at the age of ten. until then she hopes you enjoy reading the anatomy of letters unsent!

www.ingramcontent.com/pod-product-compliance
Lightning Source LLC
LaVergne TN
LVHW061343080526
838199LV00093B/6930